D0125741

The multi-talented Bruno Mars plays some sick guitar and drums.

INTRODUCTION

In 2008, Bruno Mars didn't want to go home. Back then, he was broke, trying to make it in Los Angeles. He'd almost quit many times. But one thing always stopped him: the looks he imagined on his friends' and family's faces. "I didn't want to come home to Hawaii a failure," Bruno says.

Fast forward to a happier day in December 2010. Bruno's laughing his head off. He's driving the *Whip*, his old Jeep from high school. His band buddies are with him, and he's showing them his old hangouts.

Bruno walks the red carpet at an event in December 2010.

Tomorrow, Bruno's performing at the Blaisdell arena, a nine-thousand-seat concert hall in Honolulu. At first, Bruno wasn't sure he could handle a show that big. **"But it's sold out,"** Bruno says, laying on the swag. *"Sold out."*

Next day, showtime, Bruno and his band are climbing onto the stage. They look as if they stepped out of the 1960s. They're wearing matching dark blue jackets. Bruno's hair is swept up in a classic pompadour.

POMPADOUR =
an old-fashioned hairstyle with a big pouf over the forehead

A sold-out crowd packed Blaisdell arena for Bruno's homecoming show in December 2010.

The guys step into the blinding white stage lights, and the crowd goes wild. Above the roar, you can hear the chant: "Bruno! Bruno! Bruno!"

This is how Bruno Mars wanted to go back home.

CHAPTER ONE

SHOW KID

Bruno (CENTER) with (FROM LEFT) his sister Jaime; his mom; his sister Tiara; and his brother, Eric

Bruno Mars says music is the only thing he's good at. It's the only thing he's *ever* been good at. **"I live for this,"** he told the *Los Angeles Times*. And for once, this adorably cocky crooner is not joking.

Just look at all the kinds of music he performs: pop, rock, funk, reggae, hip-hop, and R & B. He plays four instruments—guitar, drums, piano, and bass. He's gotten all kinds of awards as a performer *and* songwriter *and* producer.

Bruno says he's barely scratched the surface when it comes to music, and he should know. He's been in this biz since before he can remember.

PRODUCER =
a person whose job it is to help artists record the best music they can

Check out these "facts" Bruno's given about himself. Can you tell when this kidder is for real? Answers appear upside down below. No cheating!

1. Job he would do if he weren't a musician: cage fighter
2. Favorite way to spend a day off: doing nothing
3. Greatest fear: being attacked by panthers in his sleep
4. Favorite activity: watching music videos on YouTube
5. Favorite foods: hot sauce, grape juice, and sushi
6. Artist he'd most love to work with: Prince
7. What he does every night before going to bed: writes love songs

Answers: 1) F, 2) T, 3) F, 4) T, 5) T, 6) T, 7) F

Growing Up Onstage

Bruno was born Peter Gene Hernandez in Honolulu, Hawaii, on October 8, 1985. His mother was a singer and hula dancer from the Philippines. His Puerto Rican father was a drummer and band leader. Peter was a chubby toddler. So his father started calling him Bruno, after a famous wrestler. The nickname stuck. (Bruno added the last name Mars later because it sounded "out of this world.")

Bruno has four sisters and one brother. They all sang, but Bruno was the only one who couldn't wait to get onstage. By the age of four, he was in his father's singing group, the Love Notes. Both of his parents and his uncle performed in this doo-wop show for tourists.

DOO-WOP = a kind of simple music with catchy melodies

Bruno (IN BLUE JACKET) poses with the Love Notes including his father, Pete Hernandez (THIRD FROM RIGHT), in 2010. Bruno got his start with the doo-wop group.

Bruno's act? He fired up the crowd with his spot-on imitations of Elvis Presley.

Music was just something you did in Bruno's family. He learned to play drums, piano, and guitar without ever taking lessons. Meanwhile, he was listening to every kind of music out there.

SO ADORBS!

In 1992, Bruno took his Elvis act to the big screen. He appears for twenty short seconds in the final scene of *Honeymoon in Vegas* (RIGHT). Today, the clip is on YouTube. There's mini-Bruno in a blue sparkly jumpsuit, giant white belt, and bouncing hair. He's rockin' his bod just like the King.

By elementary school, Bruno was doing six nights a week with the Love Notes. Then, when Bruno was ten or eleven, his parents split. The family show was over, but Bruno found lots of other gigs. When he was fourteen, he wowed tourists with a Michael Jackson impersonation. Bruno raked in $200 a show, five nights a week. He was making way more than his teachers!

Two years later, Bruno was booked to be the opening act for a magic show. Night after night, he performed background music while tourists ate dinner. He also was in charge of warming up the crowd. He had to say cheesy things like, "Hey, hey, hey, aloha! Make some noise, all right?"

IMPERSONATION = a kind of act where the goal is to copy a famous performer as closely as possible

Bruno (FAR LEFT) did a killer impersonation of pop superstar Michael Jackson (LEFT) in his early teens.

"I was a circus freak," he later told interviewer Ryan Seacrest. Bruno knew there had to be a better way to do what he loved.

A Lucky Fail?

Hoping to make it for real in the music biz, Bruno made a demo to send to his sister who lived in Los Angeles. She had a contact at Motown Records who'd listen to it. Later, Bruno would joke that he sounded like Alvin the Chipmunk on that CD. But the bosses at Motown saw something special. Right after high school, Bruno moved to L.A. to become a star.

But things just didn't click in L.A. Bruno didn't know where to start or where to go. Motown dropped him a year later.

"I was too young," Bruno told interviewer Piers Morgan. **"I had so much to learn about recording."** Looking back, Bruno says that his "fail" wasn't actually a fail at all. Instead, it was a lucky break. It gave him the chance to grow as an artist. When success came, Bruno was ready for it.

Bruno in high school

DEMO =
a sample of music an artist puts together to impress a recording company

CHAPTER TWO

MAKIN' IT

Bruno (RIGHT) credits Philip Lawrence (FAR LEFT) and Ari Levine (CENTER) with helping him make it.

As it turned out, success wouldn't come for quite a while. For the next several years, Bruno was flat broke. He did whatever he could just to stay in L.A. At one point, he sold just about everything he owned—including his drums and guitar. He skipped breakfast to pay for lunch. He played in skeevy bars to ten or twenty people.

Bruno got turned down by one recording label after another. They didn't understand his music—or the color of his skin. Bruno told the *Los Angeles Times,* "You wouldn't believe how many label presidents I've heard say, 'Bruno doesn't have what it takes; we don't know how to market him, [and] we don't know what kind of music he does. You know, 'Who's this beige-looking kid with curly hair? We can't figure him out.'"

MARKET =
to promote or sell

HAT HEAD

In high school, Bruno had a huge Afro. When he chopped it off, his head felt small. So he started wearing hats. His favorite is a classic brimmed hat with a feather on the side. How many hats does Bruno own? Just six or so.

The Smeezingtons

Through it all, Bruno was growing as an artist. He wrote songs every day. By 2007, Bruno had hooked up with songwriter and singer Philip Lawrence. Phil got what Bruno was about. To this day, the two friends write everything together. Phil also sings backup in Bruno's concerts.

When sound engineer Ari Levine joined Bruno and Phil, the three became the Smeezingtons. This artistic trio is the "brains" behind Bruno. And he considers them the key to his success.

SOUND ENGINEER = the person who handles the technical part of recording music in a studio

Philip Lawrence (LEFT), Bruno, and Ari Levine (RIGHT), also known as the Smeezingtons, goof around at a Grammys event in 2011.

WHY THE NAME SMEEZINGTONS? 0_0

Bruno, Phil, and Ari were sure that each song they worked on was going to be a smash. They started calling a smash a smeeze. Why? Who knows? The guys just liked the sound of it.

What do you call guys who make smeezes? The Smeezingtons, of course! And just like that, a name was born.

The Smeezingtons pose for a portrait in their Los Angeles recording studio.

Bruno scraped money together to pay for gas just so he could get to the Smeezingtons' studio. The guys plugged away, hoping someone would listen to their music.

Growing up, Bruno spent a lot of time listening to his four sisters talk about their boyfriends. He says it's why he's able to write such amazing love songs.

Finally, a recording label bit. Executives at Epic Records were impressed by a demo the Smeezingtons had made for a song called "Lost." The only thing was, the bosses wanted to buy the song for *other* artists to perform. "I was like, 'No way...this is my art!'" Bruno told *Rolling Stone.* But then the label bosses said they'd pay $20,000 for Bruno's song. With that offer on the table, Bruno said, "'Here's your song. What else do you need?'"

Bruno (CENTER) and Philip (LEFT) didn't give up hope. They kept playing their own music too. Bruno's brother (BACKGROUND) also helped them out by playing drums onstage with them. He still does!

So Bruno and Phil started writing songs for other artists. But Bruno's feelings were mixed. It was hard for him to give away his songs. His voice was on the demo, but the final cut featured someone else. Still, Bruno was learning a ton. And he was working with top dogs in the industry. Would the right person notice him?

LOTSA DUDS

Just about anything can inspire a song for Bruno: something he's heard, a feeling, a girl. Bruno never knows what will be a hit. But he does know when he's written a bad song. Knowing when he's bombed is one of his best talents, he says.

CHAPTER THREE

JUST THE WAY HE IS

Phil and Bruno looking dapper in a 2011 performance

In early 2009, the Smeezingtons produced their first number one hit—"Right Round," performed by rapper and singer Flo Rida. That year, Bruno also worked on "Nothin' on You" for artist B.o.B. This was a rap song with a catchy, singable hook. And that hook featured the smooth sounds of Bruno Mars—even in the final cut.

HOOK =
the repeating part of a song that you can't get out of your head

Bruno performs with B.o.B. (LEFT) in 2010.

21

On the Up and Up

By spring 2010, "Nothin' on You" was a megahit. Everyone wanted to know: who *was* that talented singer with the tilted hat and to-die-for dimples?

By now, Bruno had signed a deal with Elektra Records, and he couldn't get his album out fast enough. He was in the studio almost every day from waking to sleeping.

In July, Bruno's single "Just the Way You Are" went straight to number one. Bruno wrote this sweet love song about a real girl. It was so simple that it could have been in his family's old Love Notes show. But it captured the feelings of smitten guys everywhere—and made even more girls swoon.

SINGLE = a song that is sold by itself, not as part of an album

SCREAMIN' FOR SHORTY

Bruno can't get used to girls screaming for him. It makes him laugh. "I'm three feet [0.9 meters] tall basically," he told *Spin* magazine. "What are you girls screaming at?" (For the record, Bruno is 5 feet 5 [1.7 m].)

Bruno showed his dark side with his next single, "Grenade." This song is about a guy who would die for a girl even though she doesn't love him back. With "Grenade," Bruno was already breaking records. He became the first male solo artist ever to have his first two singles go to number one.

Bruno's first solo single, "Just the Way You Are," popped up on iPods everywhere in July 2010.

SOLO =
alone, not part of a band

AN AMAZING MOMENT

Bruno played New York City for the first time in August 2010. At one point, he realized the crowd was singing his own songs back to him. It was an awesome feeling. That's when he knew he'd really made it.

Major Mistake

Then, on September 19, 2010, Bruno got a huge reality check. He had just finished a show in Vegas. He was in the casino bathroom when police came in. They caught Bruno red-handed with drugs.

Bruno doesn't talk much about the incident except to say he regrets that he did a stupid thing. Because the amount of drugs was small, Bruno didn't go to jail. He would only have to pay a fine and do volunteer work to make up for his mistake.

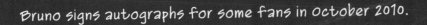

Bruno signs autographs for some fans in October 2010.

Doo-Wops & Hooligans

With his arrest, Bruno got a taste of what it felt like to be hot news for the wrong reasons. But the buzz about Bruno became positive again when his album *Doo-Wops & Hooligans* came out in October. It had ten tracks, each one very different from the next.

Still, Bruno definitely put his own stamp on each of the songs. All his stuff had simple words and tunes. Anyone could sing along. Many people said the album was a refreshing throwback. It featured real instruments instead of a computerized beat. And the vocals were all Bruno, without any help from Auto-Tune.

ALBUM = a collection of recorded songs that are sold together

Bruno holds up his album cover at the release party for *Doo-Wops & Hooligans* in 2011.

AUTO-TUNE = computer software used by many popular artists to make their voices sound better or to create a special effect

25

On the Road and Beyond

What's the downside to fame for Bruno? Not having enough time for a personal life. In 2012, Bruno said he'd been single for a long time. But would he trade in his success? Never! Bruno spent 2011 touring the planet doing what he's loved ever since he was four years old—performing live.

Bruno's stage style is just as classic as

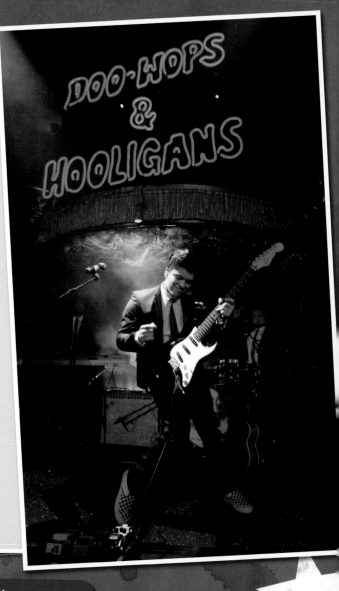

ONE LUCKY LADY

Bruno's always been super tight with his family. Early on, Bruno said his biggest dream was to make enough money so he could take care of his mother. That dream came true at the end of 2011, when he bought her a house.

everything else about him. He plays smaller halls than other big-name stars. The set and costumes are simple. None of the show has been taped beforehand.

Instead, it's Bruno and his best buds playing their hearts out. Bruno says, **"The best part of our show is that you can tell we're all friends up there, and we're having the time of our lives."**

Still, Bruno's just itching to get back in the studio and work on his next album. What can fans expect? As Bruno tweeted back in 2010, **"You ain't seen nothing yet. I've only just begun. BUCKLE UP!"**

BRUNO

PICS!

5   *Bruno Mars: Coming Home Documentary,* YouTube video, 8:20, posted by ElektraRecords, July 14, 2011, http://www.youtube.com/watch?v=W0VfyQd_PhM&feature=mfu_in_order&list=UL (February 10, 2012).

6   Ibid.

9   Matt Diehl, "Bruno Mars' Astronomical Success," *Los Angeles Times,* February 6, 2011, http://www.latimes.com/entertainment/news/music/la-ca-bruno-mars-20110206,0,7351623.story (February 10, 2012).

10   Ibid.

13   "Bruno Mars Interview Just Before Arrest," YouTube video, 8:36, posted by ryanseacrest, September 17, 2010, http://www.youtube.com/watch?v=GeBIBPpy2KY (February 10, 2012).

13   "Bruno Mars Dropped from Motown Records, Interview with Piers Morgan," CNN video, 2:46, January 10, 2012, http://www.cnn.com/video/#/video/bestoftv/2012/01/06/piers-morgan-bruno-mars-motown.cnn (February 10, 2012).

15   Diehl, "Bruno Mars."

18   Jonah Weiner, "Mr. Showbiz," *Rolling Stone,* January 20, 2011, http://www.ebscohost.com (January 31, 2012).

22   Christopher R. Weingarten, "Bruno Mars & Janelle Monae Chat Backstage," *Spin,* May 11, 2011, http://www.spin.com/articles/bruno-mars-janelle-monae-chat-backstage (February 10, 2012).

27   *Bruno Mars: Coming Home Documentary.*

27   Bruno Mars, Twitter, http://twitter.com/#!/brunomars, posted on October 11, 2010.

Bruno Mars Official Site
http://www.brunomars.com
Bruno's site has the most up-to-date Hooligans news online. You'll also find awesome live concert videos. While you're there, join Bruno's fan club and check out the funky, retro stuff for sale.

Krohn, Katherine. *Michael Jackson: Ultimate Music Legend.* Minneapolis: Lerner Publications Company, 2010. Read all about Michael Jackson—the King of Pop whom Bruno Mars used to imitate as a teen.

Landau, Elaine. *Is Singing for You?* Minneapolis: Lerner Publications Company, 2011. Do you dream of making it big in the music biz like Bruno? Find out what it takes to make it as a singer.

"Little Elvis" Scene from *Honeymoon in Vegas* (1992)
http://www.youtube.com/watch?v=BFDcVvDB1Ko
You *gotta* check out Bruno singing Elvis at the age of six. Too cute!

Stamaty, Mark Alan. *Shake, Rattle & Turn That Noise Down!: How Elvis Shook Up Music, Me, & Mom.* New York: Knopf, 2010.
This kids' book about loving Elvis could have been written by Bruno himself.

INDEX

PHOTO ACKNOWLEDGMENTS

The images in this book are used with the permission of: © George Pimentel/WireImage/Getty Images, pp. 2, 27; © Catherine McGann/Hulton Archive/Getty Images, pp. 3 (top), 8 (top); © Michael Buckner/WireImage/Getty Images, pp. 3 (bottom), 28 (top left), 28 (bottom); Oscar A. Hernandez - Photographer (InfinityPacificPhoto.com), pp. 4 (both), 6; © Mike Coppola/FilmMagic/Getty Images, p. 5; © Aaron Yoshino, p. 7; © Joefer Bautista, p. 8 (bottom); © Peter Kramer/NBC/NBCU Photo Bank via Getty Images, p. 9; Honolulu Star-Advertiser, pp. 11 (top), 12 (left); © Columbia Pictures/Photofest, p. 11 (bottom); © CBS Photo Archive/Getty Images, p. 12 (right); Seth Poppel Yearbook Library, p. 13; © Alberto E. Rodriguez/Getty Images, pp. 14 (top), 24; AP Photo/Chris Pizzello, pp. 14 (bottom), 17; © Lester Cohen/WireImage/Getty Images, p. 15; © Steve Granitz/WireImage/Getty Images, p. 16; © Jared Milgrim/CORBIS, p. 18; © Alberto E. Rodriguez/WireImage/Getty Images, p. 19; © Theo Wargo/WireImage/Getty Images, p. 20 (top); © Jeff Kravitz/FilmMagic/Getty Images, p. 20 (bottom left); AP Photo/Matt Sayles, p. 20 (bottom right); © Kevin Winter/Getty Images, p. 21; © Featureflash/Dreamstime.com, p. 22; © Todd Strand/Independent Picture Service, p. 23; © David J Hogan/Getty Images, pp. 25, 26; © C Flanigan/FilmMagic/Getty Images, p. 28 (top right); © Simone Joyner/Getty Images, p. 29 (top left); © Jason Merritt/Getty Images, p. 29 (top center); © Frank Hoensch/Getty Images, p. 29 (right); © Cliff Lipson/CBS Photo Archive/Getty Images, p. 29 (bottom).

Front cover: © John Shearer/WireImage/Getty Images (left); © Angela Weiss/WireImage/Getty Images (right).

Back cover: © Jason Merritt/Getty Images.

Main body text set in Shannon Std Book 12/18.
Typeface provided by Monotype Typography.